Dedication

To my Mom, **Marj Gross**,
my greatest supporter in life and business,
whose radiant smile and positive outlook remind me daily
of what it means to choose joy.

To **Barbara Hemphill**,
my greatest mentor, whose faith, courage, and vision have inspired
hope in thousands, transforming not just my life, but the lives of
countless others who now carry her light forward.

To **Demetrius Farrior**,
my greatest friend, whose quiet strength and steadfast consistency
have been a steady compass on my journey.

To our **Certified Productive Environment Specialists**,
who carry this message into the world with wisdom and grace.

To **Edz and Yuliana**,
our amazing team who keep Productive Environment Institute moving forward and take such good care of our clients with dedication
and heart.

To our **SOAR to Success Members**,
whose courage to create order and freedom is a constant reminder
of why this work matters.

And to **Buddy and Charlie**,
my faithful four-legged friends,
who remind me that rest, play, and presence
are essential parts of a productive environment. ☺

Testimonials

FROM CLUTTER TO CLARITY by Gina
A Story of Determination and Discovery

My journey to PEI, perhaps like many others, has been a long one. But it's a journey marked by perseverance and deep conviction. I always believed that the people around me had figured it out: how to stay organized, how to stay on top of their game, how to succeed in life. And if it was possible for them, it had to be possible for me... I just didn't have the right tools.

After college and graduate school, I stepped into the real world and quickly realized I needed real-world skills. I began devouring the books I thought would help, titles like *The 7 Habits of Highly Effective People* by Stephen Covey. I even enrolled in SkillPath Seminars and took correspondence courses (as they were called back then) to reinforce what I was learning. I completed those courses. I earned the certificates. But I couldn't translate those principles into consistent action. Despite my desire and efforts, the systems didn't stick.

Over time, life continued, and so did the accumulation of papers, books, and records. The stacks grew taller, the boxes multiplied. I often joked that I was the archaeologist of my own life...because only I knew where things were buried. And even then, finding what I needed was never easy.

Fast forward nearly thirty years: everything changed when I met Barbara and Andrea and enrolled in their workshop at the Productive Environment Institute. Their approach wasn't just theory. It was practical, tangible, doable. The systems they teach actually *work*, and more importantly, they *fit* the way I think and live.

As I began sorting through my files and applying the PEI methods, something amazing happened: I came across those old SkillPath certificates, the ones I had earned decades ago. But this time, I didn't stumble across them by accident. I found them with a single click of the keyboard. They were right where they belonged, because I now had a system that made retrieval simple.

I can't fully express the joy I felt in that moment. Not just for finding a long-lost document, but for finding myself capable. I felt relief, clarity, and pride. My thinking was no longer clouded by chaos. My space felt lighter. My mind felt freer. And most of all, I realized: the potential had always been there. I just needed a path to unlock it.

DENISE'S DISCOVERY
A Seasoned Organizer Finds a Smarter Way to Search

If you deal with paper piles, clutter, or even digital chaos, the Productive Environment Finding SYSTEM™ will change everything. Truly, if you've ever spent more than a minute searching for something, this is for you.

As a professional organizer with over four decades of experience, I've seen how frustrating it can be to waste time looking for things you *know* you have, but just can't put your hands on. In the past, I helped clients create detailed paper lists to track their files. It worked, kind of. But it doesn't come close to what this system offers.

What I love most is the flexibility. There's more than one way to track and retrieve what you need, digitally or on paper, which makes it practical for *real* life. You can make it your own and scale it as you go. After all these years helping others get organized, I've *never* been this excited about a method for managing information. The PEI system doesn't just organize your files, it gives you back your peace of mind.

When I first heard Barbara say the system "gets stronger with use," I didn't fully understand. But now I do, it's like building a muscle. The more you use it, the easier it becomes. Each time you retrieve something quickly or add something thoughtfully, you reinforce your confidence. It's reliable. It's empowering. And it builds momentum in a way I haven't experienced with any other method.

So if you're sitting in overwhelm, surrounded by paper or digital files, or even if you think you've tried it all, I encourage you to give this system a try. I have a feeling you'll wonder, like I did, how you ever managed without it.

FROM OVERWHELM TO OPEN SPACE by Nancy
A SOAR Client's Journey

I found Barbara Hemphill on YouTube during one of my late-night searches for help. Organizing… search. Tidying up… search. Hoarding… search. I was drowning in papers, memories, and "stuff" from over 50 years of living in the same space. I wasn't just looking for advice, I was looking for hope.

I'd tried before. Bought organizing books, made progress, then stalled. When I sold a house with a five-car garage, I cleared some things, but mostly just moved the clutter with me. Anyone who saves things knows: extra storage is a blessing and a trap.

Then I discovered the Productive Environment Institute. Even the name lifted my spirits. I signed up for a Bootcamp with Barbara and Andrea. Their tagline, "Accomplish your work. Enjoy your life", felt like a lifeline. I joined their Digital Organizing class in late summer 2024, even though I barely understood what a drive was or where my downloads went. I just clicked around until I found what I needed, if I was lucky.

But as I began to sort digital clutter, I realized my heart was pulling me toward the physical piles, on my desk, in drawers, closets, photo boxes. So many items, stuffed everywhere. Sentimental, over-whelming, and silently stealing my space and energy.

At Barbara and Andrea's suggestion, I started with what was new, today's emails, today's mail. It helped. I got more intentional about what I let in. I used to keep things just because they'd "been around." Now I saw how they became part of the clutter family.

A family reunion in May gave me a reason to dig deeper. I sorted through decades of saved articles and memorabilia from our candy store. Five large boxes became 23 manila folders, one for each family member. Traditional Austrian clothing I had worn in the shop was hung for my granddaughters to choose from. It was healing.

I tackled the garage. What had been chaos became a neat row of labeled bins. Not perfect, but walkable, and no longer a source of shame. I spruced up the yard. Inside, the house began to feel lighter, more peaceful. Still full of meaning, but no longer packed tight.

Something unexpected happened: as I cleared the clutter, my vision returned. My energy came back. I began doing the things I love again, the things I always said I'd get to once I got organized. The SOAR community encouraged me. I wasn't alone. We're all in this together, learning to let go and move forward.

The clutter had been a buffer, protecting me from facing deeper fears and dreams. Now, I'm choosing freedom instead.

In making space around me, you helped me find something even greater, peace, hope, and the beginning of something new.

Table of Contents

Foreword

I am thankful and humbled to write the Foreword for this book. Over 30 years ago, I took a selling course taught by a man who had already been gone for a decade, yet his voice lived on through audio-cassette tapes. In that moment, I set a goal: to create something that would outlive me and continue helping others long after I'd gone to my heavenly home. Thanks to my long-time friend and colleague, Andrea Anderson, that dream has become a reality.

Andrea and I began working together in 2005. We often joke that we go together like "Peanut Butter" and "Jelly." I've always loved the big picture, while Andrea has the rare gift of turning vision into systems that actually work. Her genius lies in making ideas not only possible but practical, moving them forward in ways I could never have imagined.

People who know me well know that I have struggled with depression since childhood, which has shaped much of my entrepreneurial journey. There were times I was ready to give up. On several of those occasions, Andrea's steady belief and practical support kept me going. Without her, I have no doubt I would have walked away. Because of her, I continue to serve, and I can trust that the legacy we've built will endure.

Both of us started our careers as teachers, but Andrea's experience in education and mental health gave her a deep compassion for people who feel overwhelmed. Together, we discovered that organizing and productivity is more than checklists and calendars, it is truly an *art*.

Through the years we've learned that three elements are essential for lasting success:

1. A **SYSTEM** (Saving You Space, Time, Energy, and Money)
2. **Accountability**
3. **Community**

Andrea embodies all three. In 2018, she created our vibrant community Productive Environment Network™. In 2024, she created The SOAR Board™, a digital evolution of my first published product, *The "To Do" Book*. This tool is the bridge between physical information and digital information - and helps you *find* anything you file, online or on paper, in seconds!

At no time in history has the need been greater. With the flood of information, now magnified by artificial intelligence, managing time, space, and information is no longer optional. It's essential.

If you remember only one truth from this book, let it be this: **Clutter is postponed decisions®**. Making those decisions is rarely easy, but Andrea has proven again and again that with the right tools and support, you can do it.

As you read these pages, don't postpone. Later always costs more, in time, money, energy, and opportunity. Take the first step now, and let Andrea guide you.

You will discover that you truly *can* accomplish your work and enjoy your life.

BARBARA HEMPHILL
Founder, Productive Environment Institute

Introduction

When I first met Barbara Hemphill in 2005, I had no idea how much that connection would shape the rest of my life. At the time, I was working for a family preservation agency and had a smart, successful boss named Debbie. She was deeply committed to her work, and like many professionals at that time, her work was paper-intensive. Stacks of documents filled her desk and office floor.

We lived 3.5 hours apart and she'd often say "You need to come here and get me organized!" So I would spend days, even weeks, trying to bring order to her papers with traditional filing systems. Everything looked neat when I left. But the moment she returned from a business trip, she would sigh and say, "Well, it looks great, but I can't find anything."

One afternoon, after yet another attempt had unraveled, I sat at her desk in tears. In my frustration I prayed, "God, there has got to be a better way!" Moments later, I typed "filing system" into Google. The very first result was *Barbara Hemphill, the "Paper Tiger Lady"*, and her system *Taming the Paper Tiger*. That discovery changed everything.

Barbara's system was different. Instead of relying on traditional alphabetical order or complex categories that no one could remember, she introduced a **numerical <u>finding</u> system** supported by a simple index. Intrigued, I ordered the materials right away, studied how the system worked, and then set it up for Debbie's office. For the first time, every piece of paper had a clear place to go, and a reliable way to find it again.

I could file things quickly, and more importantly, *Debbie could find them in seconds!* It worked.

That was the beginning of my journey. Within a year, I connected with Barbara, joined her team, quit my job and launched my own organizing business. Not long after, Barbara invited me into the opportunity of a lifetime: to partner with her in carrying her vision forward. What began as a mentorship became a true collaboration, and together we continued refining the systems she pioneered.

Nearly twenty years later, Barbara and I made an exciting discovery together. The SOAR Board™, the digital tool I created to help professionals manage *both paper and digital* information with Barbara's principles, was in many ways, the modern version of her original *"To Do" Book* she created in 1983...when I was in the 7th grade!

The SOAR Board™ is more than an evolution. It is the only tool that truly integrates physical and digital information into one system. With the File Index built directly into the SOAR Board™, someone can find a piece of paper in their physical filing cabinet just as quickly as they could locate a digital file on their computer.

That realization confirmed what we both knew: this was revolutionary.

Barbara has always been the face of the Productive Environment Institute. Her story, her faith, and her passion launched an entire industry of organizing and productivity professionals. She has written the Foreword to this book, sharing part of her journey in her own words. But this Introduction is about what happens when two stories intersect, her legacy and my calling. I believe God orchestrated that moment at Debbie's desk in 2005 so that I could carry forward Barbara's vision into the next generation.

And that is what this book is about: equipping you with a system that works, not just for paper, not just for email, not just for "stuff," but for all the information in your life.

If you are like many of our community members, you are a successful professional or business owner. Maybe you are retired now but managing your own affairs and, increasingly, the affairs of an aging parent. You are bright, capable, and hardworking. But your desk has piles of paper, your inbox is overflowing, and your hard drive looks like a digital junk drawer. You have tried different systems before. Some worked for a while, but none of them lasted. And in the quiet moments, you wonder: *Is this just how it has to be?*

The answer is no.

What you are about to discover is not just another set of tips and tricks. It is a comprehensive system built on three levels:

- **Methodology**: understanding the big picture so you choose tools and processes that actually fit *your* life.
- **Mechanics**: step-by-step strategies to create a repeatable SYSTEM™ (Saving You Space, Time, Energy, and Money).
- **Maintenance**: building habits and support structures that keep the system going, long after the initial burst of motivation has faded.

This is the part most people miss. They think if they just buy the right software, download the right app, or rearrange their files one more time, everything will fall into place. But real transformation requires all three levels. That is why our community and programs exist, to help you learn, apply, and sustain your success.

A quick note on language:

Throughout this book, I use two related terms intentionally. The SOAR Method™ refers to the underlying methodology, the way of thinking and making decisions about information, time, and priorities. The SOAR to Success System™ refers to the complete framework taught in this book, where the method is applied through specific tools, structures, and routines. The SOAR to Success System™ is also the name of our flagship program, where members receive coaching, support, and community to fully implement and sustain what you're learning here.

Will this work overnight? No. Change takes time, intention, and practice. But if you are willing to lean in, what feels impossible today will become second nature tomorrow. You will go from frustrated to focused, inundated to in control, and overwhelmed to optimized.

Most of all, I want you to feel hopeful again. You *can* accomplish your work and enjoy your life. You do not have to be buried under clutter, distracted by digital chaos, or weighed down by the nagging fear that something important has slipped through the cracks.

That is why this book exists. To offer you a way forward. To honor Barbara's legacy. And to invite you into a system and a community where you are not alone, because we believe *Together, We Are Better!*

Let's begin.

— ANDREA ANDERSON

Chapter 1

Foundation

From Confusion to Clarity with the Productive Environment Finding SYSTEM™

If you've ever stared at a stack of papers thinking, "I don't even know where to start...", you've come to the right place.

Before we get to labels, inboxes, or checklists, we need to start with the foundation: how you think about information.

Because that's what this is really about, making decisions and retrieving what you need *when* you need it. Whether it's a bill, a client file, or your car title, your productivity depends on one thing: **how quickly you can find your stuff.**

Barbara's Journey: The Birth of the File Index

In 1978, Barbara Hemphill began working with families and small businesses to organize their filing systems. Her early method was simple and familiar: alphabetical folders with plastic file tabs, staggered neatly in a drawer. It worked, until it didn't.

"One person labeled a file 'Car,'" she recalls, "but their spouse was looking for it under 'Honda' or 'Vehicle.'"

That's when she realized: **It's not enough to name a file. We need to make it *findable,* for anyone.**

Barbara began writing the file names on a yellow legal pad, so others could see what existed and avoid duplicating files. That became her first **File Index**, and what she discovered was revolutionary:

A File Index is to filing what a Chart of Accounts is to accounting.

From Paper Cuts to Productivity

Eventually, Barbara moved her File Index from paper to Microsoft Word, then to Excel, and later helped develop software that allowed people to "Google their filing cabinets."

What began as a handwritten list became the **Productive Environment Finding SYSTEM™**, a keyword-driven structure that works across any industry, household, or team. The result?

A life where paper (and digital) files serve you, not stress you out.

Think Google, But for Paper

If you've ever used Google (who hasn't?!), you already understand the Finding SYSTEM™.

You type in a keyword, and up pops what you're looking for. It doesn't matter where that document "lives." The system retrieves it.

That's the power of a keyword-driven File Index. And instead of spending energy trying to remember where you filed something, you simply search.

The Two Filing Types: Action & Reference

In our system, there are only two kinds of files:
- **Action Files** – for active, in-progress work (think: current clients, bills to pay, ongoing projects)
- **Reference Files** – for information you want to keep but don't use every day

Both types are numbered (e.g., Action 1–25, Reference 1–100). You maintain one single File Index for each, that links file numbers to keywords.

This eliminates:
- Confusion about what to name a file
- Wasted time searching through folders
- The fear of tossing something you might need later

Why the System Works

Let's be honest: most people don't mind filing, they mind *not being able to find what they filed.*

Our system solves that.

You no longer need to decide *where* something goes. You just need to label it with keywords, assign it a number, and log it in the index. Anyone, even a family member or team assistant, can retrieve it later.

Physical vs. Digital Files: A Strategic Shift

We teach a **numerical system** for physical paper because the drawers don't have search bars.

But for digital files, we recommend an **ABC folder structure**, because search *is* built-in, and alphabetical filing is easier to maintain electronically.

It's not about one-size-fits-all. It's about **filing based on how you <u>find</u>.**

📌 Client Snapshot: Anne's Filing Turnaround

Anne, a retired educator, came to us with six drawers of paper and no clear system. She was overwhelmed, especially after moving and combining years of files from two different homes.

Once we set up her Reference Files with numbers and added keywords like insurance, Blue Cross, auto policy, Anne lit up:

> *"I've had these files for 20 years and could never find what I needed. Now I can find it in seconds."*

She printed her File Index and placed it at the front of her file drawer, and keeps a digital copy in her SOAR Board™ so it's even searchable on her phone.

What You Need to Know

The File Index is the foundation of your entire system. Without it, you're managing chaos. With it, you're building confidence.

- This chapter introduced the concept, but you'll get full setup instructions in Chapter 5.
- You can use the File Index for more than just paper. It works for storage, memorabilia, binders, and even client documents.

Coming Up in Chapter 2

We'll introduce the Magic 7™,
the seven essential tools you
need in place before organizing
anything else.

Chapter 2

Equip

From Unequipped to Equipped

*"I've tried to get organized, but I never seem to have
what I need when I sit down to work."*

That's because most people try to start organizing without first putting the right tools in place. But organizing without equipping yourself is like building a house without a hammer. It simply doesn't work.

This chapter is about the **seven essential tools** you need in your workspace to create and sustain a productive environment.

We call them the **Magic 7™,** and adding that seventh tool changed everything.

The Story Behind the Magic

Before the software, the workshops, and the books, Barbara Hemphill was in the field, working side by side with hundreds of people in homes and offices. She was always adapting her approach to suit individual needs.

But over time, a pattern emerged.

"Whether someone was an attorney, an artist, or a stay-at-home parent, the ones who made lasting progress all had the same basic tools in place," Barbara recalls.

"So I created a checklist of the must-haves."

For years, that checklist became the Magic 6™, a set of core tools that helped people organize their information and make better decisions. But as the work world changed, something became clear: our system didn't yet include a way to manage tasks and projects in context. People weren't struggling because they lacked to-do lists. They had plenty: notebooks, planners, apps, sticky notes, email flags, reminders.

The real issue was that their tasks lived outside the structure we were helping them build. Their information was getting organized... but their actions weren't connected to it. Nothing linked what they needed to do with the place where their notes, documents, and decisions lived.

We realized we were asking clients to navigate two disconnected worlds:

- The world where they stored information.
- And the world where they managed what to do with it.

That's when we knew the Magic 6™ needed a seventh tool.

Not because people didn't have task systems, but because we didn't yet offer a task-and-project system that fit within the larger context of a productive environment.

The **SOAR Board™** became that missing link, the tool that brought everything together so tasks, projects, notes, and decisions could finally live in one integrated system.

With that addition, the Magic 6™ became the Magic 7™, a complete, cohesive set of tools that supports how people actually think, work, and take action.

The Magic 7™ Tools

Here's what every productive workspace needs, whether you're working at a kitchen table or in a corner office.

---

1. In / Out / File Trays

We recommend a 3-tier tray system on or near your desk.

Think of it as a landing zone, instead of letting things pile up on every flat surface.

The top "In" tray is where all incoming paper lands *before* you make decisions.

In Tray – for anything unprocessed

Out Tray – for items leaving your space

To File – for anything that needs to go into Action or Reference Files later

Set it up now, and your desk will instantly feel lighter.

---

2. Toss / Recycle / Shred

This one seems obvious, but it's often overlooked.

You need:

- A trash can (ideally within arm's reach)
- A recycle bin or paper reuse tray
- A shredder (or a folder labeled "To Shred")

When you start sorting your "In" tray, you'll realize how much can be tossed immediately, if the tools are nearby.

---

3. Calendar / Planner

We don't prescribe a specific calendar app or planner, because the best system is the one *you'll actually use*. What we teach is **ownership**:

Taking responsibility for choosing a tool, committing to it, and using it consistently, not just when you're overwhelmed or behind. Whether it's paper or digital, your calendar becomes a tool of *intention* when you use it to proactively plan, protect, and align your time with your priorities.

We'll cover physical vs digital calendars, time blocking and planning routines in Chapter 7. For now, make sure you at least have a basic calendar you can easily refer to.

---

4. Contact Relationship Manager (CRM)

This can be as simple as your phone's address book, a physical address book, an excel spreadsheet, or a robust system like PEconnect™, our CRM, powered by High Level.

The point is: you need a place to store names, emails, phone numbers, and notes about the people in your life and business.

If you've ever scribbled a number on a napkin and then lost it, or returned from a networking event with a pile of business cards never to be touched again... this one's for you.

---

5. Action System

This is where most people encounter difficulty.

When paper comes in that requires a task (pay, call, research, decide), it doesn't belong in a pile, it belongs in your **Action System.**

We recommend setting up a few folders labeled:
- Bills to Pay
- Calls to Make
- Waiting on Response
- Projects by Name

You'll learn to file Projects using the same numerical method we teach for Reference Files in Chapter 5. For now, start gathering items that need your attention.

---

6. Reference System

This is your long-term storage, your "I might need it someday" files.

Reference files can live across the room or in a closet, because you don't need them daily. But they still need to be organized so you can retrieve them fast.

We'll show you exactly how to set this up, step-by-step, in Chapter 5 using our proprietary Finding System, aka File Index method..

7. Integrated Task Manager (The SOAR Board™)

This was the turning point.

Adding a Task Manager to the Magic 6™ was the moment everything clicked. It wasn't enough to capture papers or organize files, we needed a central hub to **manage the work itself**.

That's when the **SOAR Board™** powered by WorkFlowy® was born. It bridges the gap between paper and digital, and between making lists and actually getting things done.

It brings together your:
- Calendar
- Projects
- Daily actions
- Follow-ups
- Reference items

... all into one easy-to-use dashboard.

Introducing The SOAR Board™

Barbara Hemphill's philosophy regarding "Taming the Paper Tiger", is about managing all information effectively, whether it's on paper or online.

By extending this approach to the digital space, the SOAR Board™ provides a consistent framework (Systemize & Organize w/ Action & Reference) that parallels your physical setup. You always know exactly where to put things, physically or digitally, and how to FIND them when needed.

The SOAR Board™ serves as your digital dashboard, or command center, mirroring Productive Environment Institute's proven strategies for organizing both physical and digital information.

SOAR to Success with the SOAR Board™
- **Systemize** the Capture of Information
- **Organize** the Information You Capture
- **Action** - Stay on Top of Projects & Tasks (aka To Do Items)
- **Reference** (File) - Find Anything You File in Seconds (including paper!)

Systemize & Organize w/ Action & Reference

With the SOAR Board™, you have a clear, adaptable system that helps you manage every aspect of your life, ensuring nothing falls through the cracks, and you can find anything you file (or store) in seconds!

The SOAR Board™ is a strategic productivity tool designed to help you capture, organize, and act on both physical and digital information, while also providing a reliable system for future reference. Its four core principles ensure that every project, task, note, or idea has a clear place and purpose.

Systemize the Capture of Information

Create a consistent method for gathering incoming tasks and ideas, whether they originate from email, handwritten notes, or other sources.

Physical Inbox and Digital Inbox
- Just as you'll have a physical inbox for incoming mail and paper-based information, you'll also have a digital inbox in your SOAR Board™ for capturing tasks, ideas, and other electronic information.
- Any paper items that enter your workspace go into the physical inbox, ensuring nothing gets lost. Likewise, your digital inbox in your SOAR Board™ receives all incoming information that appears online, via email or in your mind.

Various sources of incoming information

Organize the Information

Sort and categorize the items you captured in your Inbox into either Action or Reference.

- **Action (Act)** is when the ball is in your court to do something. It's a "To Do" or a "Task" that needs to be completed.
- **Reference (File)** is information that does not require an Action, but you want to File for future Reference.

Various sources of incoming information, sorted by things that require action, or things to file for future reference.

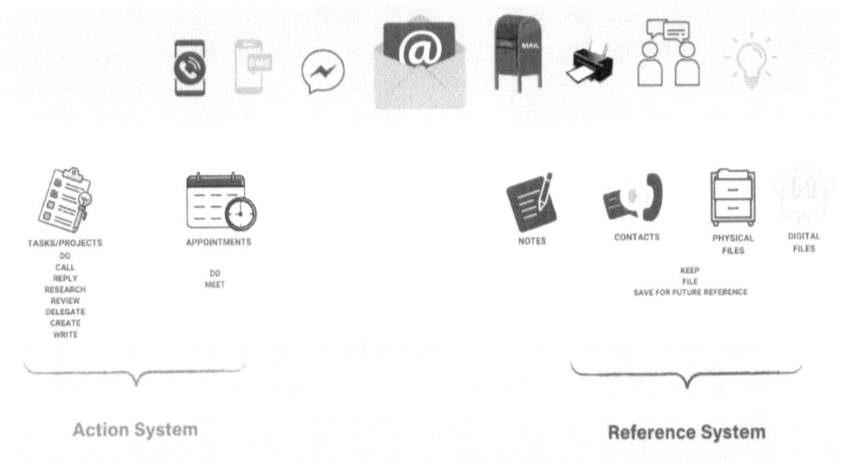

Action System

Items identified as needing action in the physical world match the "Action" or "Tasks" sections in the SOAR Board™. All other Actions or Tasks are also added to the SOAR Board™ as one of 3 types of Actions - by Date, by Type, or by Project.

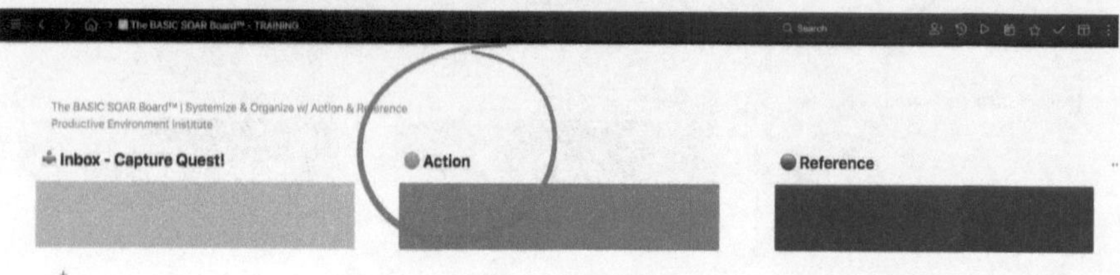

Various sources of incoming information, sorted by things that require action, then sorted further by type of Action.

Reference System

Maintain a dedicated space for storing information that must be kept for future reference, so you can retrieve it quickly when needed, as well as quick access to other resources, all in one place.

- Documents sorted to "Reference" go into your physical filing system, file folders, binders, or cabinets, and are indexed in your SOAR Board™ File Index for Physical Files - PEI's secret sauce!

- In the digital world, scanned documents or related files and links are stored in the "Reference" section of your **SOAR Board™ for Digital Files**, forming another crucial part of your **Productive Environment Finding System™**, so you can easily find what you need when you need it.

Various sources of incoming information, sorted by things that require action, or things to file for future reference; then sorted further by type of Action (by date, by type, by project); and type of Reference (notes, contacts, physical files, digital files)

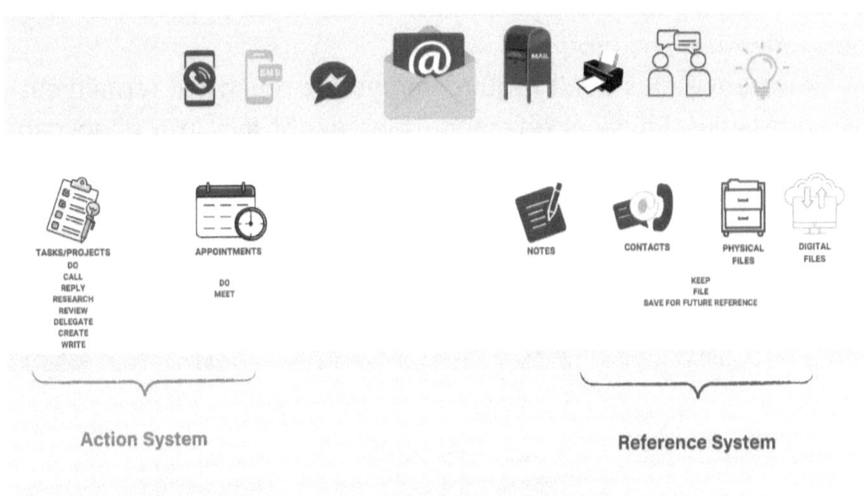

📌 Client Snapshot: Paula's Magic 7™ Moment

Paula is a busy entrepreneur, mom, and homeschool leader. When we first met, her workspace was overflowing, not with clutter, but with tools that didn't work together.

A calendar on her fridge. Tasks in a planner. Email alerts everywhere. A drawer of paper marked "URGENT", but untouched for months.

Once we helped her set up the Magic 7™, and installed the SOAR Board™ as her task manager and digital dashboard, something clicked.

> *"It wasn't that I didn't know what to do, it was that I didn't have a place to put it all. Now that I do, my brain finally gets a break."*

A Word About Placement

The first five tools (In/Out/File, Toss, Calendar, CRM, and Action) belong within arm's reach of your desk, whether they're physical tools or digital equivalents, to support daily workflow with minimal friction.

The Task Manager (Actions inside your SOAR Board™) lives on your computer and stays just a click away for quick access to projects, priorities, and progress.

Reference files don't require immediate reach but remain easily accessible. Physical reference files might live in a filing cabinet across the room, while digital reference files are stored in organized folders, cloud storage, and your SOAR Board™. Both systems play a vital role, and both need to be trusted, maintained, and used consistently.

Coming Up in Chapter 3

We'll teach you how to process all that incoming information using our signature ART of Organizing Information™ framework, and make clutter disappear, fast.

Flow

From Bottleneck to Easy Flow

*"I have so many piles... and I don't even know what's
in them."*

If that feels familiar, take a deep breath, because this is the chapter where the clutter begins to disappear.

You've started equipping your workspace using the Magic 7™. You've got the right tools in place. Now it's time to create **flow**, the smooth movement of information into and through your system.

And the secret to creating flow isn't color-coded folders or perfect labels.

It all comes down to making confident decisions.

Practice the ART of Organizing Information™

We define information broadly: paper, emails, notes, voicemails, digital downloads, screenshots, receipts, meeting agendas. It's all information, and it's all coming at you every day.

To manage it, we teach a method called **The ART of Organizing Information™**, a universal decision-making system that works no matter what kind of clutter you're facing.

ART stands for:

- **A = Action** – I need to do something with this
- **R = Reference** – I need to keep it, but no action is required
- **T = Toss** – I don't need or want this anymore

Clutter doesn't come from having too much information, it's caused by postponed decisions. And The ART of Organizing Information™ gives you a framework for moving every item forward.

The ART of Organizing Paper™

Let's start with your physical environment.

You probably have stacks, piles, and paper "to deal with." Most people do. Instead of filing first, we recommend a **First Sort** using The ART of Organizing Paper™.

Here's how:

1. **Create three categories or piles:**
   - **Action**
   - **Reference**
   - **Toss**
2. **Pick up one item at a time**, and ask: What does this require from me?
3. **Sort it based on ART,** don't try to file yet. Just make the first decision.

Examples:

- A bill you haven't paid → **Action**
- Your child's report card → **Reference**
- An expired flyer → **Toss**

This simple exercise clears the fog and gives you momentum. Often, clients find that 50% or more of their piles go straight to Toss, they just never stopped to decide.

The ART of Organizing Email™

You can use the same framework with your email inbox.

Create two folders or labels in your email platform:

- **Action** – for emails that need a reply or task
- **Reference** – for info to keep (receipts, confirmations, PDFs)
- **Toss** – for anything that's no longer needed, just delete!

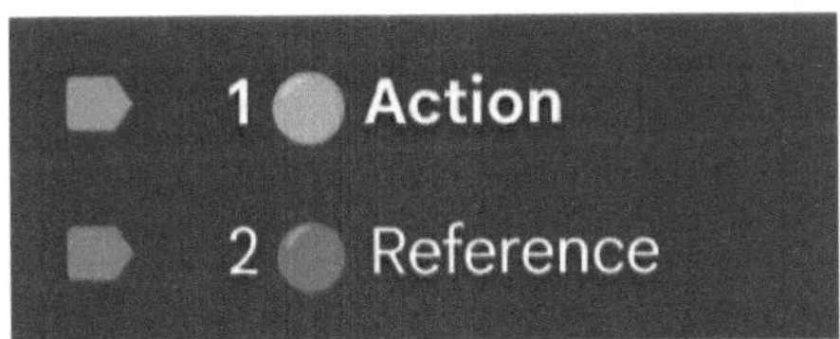

Every time a new email comes in, apply ART. Stop re-reading the same message five times before doing anything with it.

We'll dive deeper into email management in Chapter 6, but you can begin today by practicing the ART of Organizing Email™ to sort your inbox right now.

The ART of Organizing Digital Information™

This applies to everything stored on your computer or in the cloud, including your Downloads folder.

Start by creating two folders: **Action** and **Reference** on your computer first.

You'll use these as your temporary sorting zones as you begin organizing.

Then, take a small batch of files and ask:

- Is this something I need to act on soon? → Move it to **Action**
- Is it something I want to keep for future reference? → Move it to **Reference**
- Don't need it? → Delete it. (That's your **Toss**.)

Once you've created the folders on your computer, do the same for any cloud drives you have such as Google Drive or Dropbox.

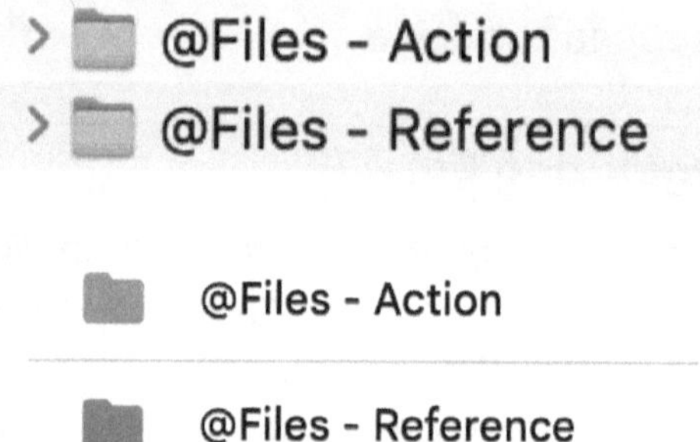

You'll learn how to structure these folders for the long term in Chapter 6. For now, just practice making decisions and moving files into their place.

📌 Client Snapshot: Cheryl's Desk Breakthrough

When Cheryl joined the SOAR to Success program, she had 17 piles on her dining room table. Most had been there for months, some, for years.

She blocked off two hours, grabbed sticky notes labeled A, R, and T... and began sorting.

"I didn't file anything. I didn't throw anything away yet. But for the first time in years, I knew what everything was."

That evening, she sat at her table, clear and clean, and ate dinner with her family. It wasn't just about decluttering. It was about getting her *space* and *clarity* back.

Start Here. Then Structure.

You can't organize what you haven't processed.

The ART of Organizing Information is how you make decisions *before* you try to store anything. It's like dumping out the pieces of a jigsaw puzzle. You need to flip them over and sort the edges before you can start building the picture.

Once your items are sorted into Action, Reference, or Toss, you're ready to start building structure with your SOAR Board™, Magic 7™ tools, and filing systems.

We'll show you how to create your Action system using three simple strategies: by Date, by Type, and by Project.

Chapter 4

Act

From Postponed to Planned

"I'm afraid I'll forget something important... so I keep everything in sight."

If that sounds familiar, you're not alone. It's a common practice, but it backfires.

The more you keep in view, the more overwhelmed your brain becomes.

The real problem isn't remembering what to do. It's not having a trusted place to track and manage Action items.

This chapter shows you how to create that system, one that supports you daily, and gets more valuable the more you use it.

From Decision to Action

In Chapter 3, you learned how to use **The ART of Organizing Information™** to process incoming information, deciding whether each item is an **Action**, a **Reference**, or belongs in the **Toss** pile.

Now it's time to focus on everything in the **Action** category.

This is where follow-through happens, not because you work harder, but because your system supports your focus. And whether you're working with paper or digital tools, your **SOAR Board™** becomes your hub.

Three Ways to Organize Action Items

Most Action items fall into one of three categories:

1. By Date

This method is for anything with a deadline, time trigger, or scheduled follow-up.

Examples:
- Bills due on the 15th
- Call scheduled for next Tuesday
- A reminder to renew your passport next month

In your **SOAR Board™**, this structure lives under **"Actions by Date"**, a single bullet that contains a timeline -a simple list of upcoming days such as Thu Jan 1, Fri Jan 2, Sat Jan 3...included in your SOAR Board™ template.

You can also use the list of upcoming days format physically with a system we call the **Swiftfile Solution™**, explained soon.

2. By Type (Permanent Actions)

These are recurring categories of work, actions you take often, no matter the project.

Examples:
- "Bills to Pay"
- "Receipts to Process"
- "Waiting on Response"
- "Calls to Make"
- "Discuss with [Name]"

In the section on your SOAR Board™ labeled **"Permanent Actions"**, add a bullet for each type that applies to you. These categories rarely change, but the content within them will.

In a physical system, you might use 3-5 folders for these and keep them near your Swiftfile™ or in a top drawer for easy access.

3. By Project or Topic

Most of our lives and businesses are built around projects, things we're building, solving, delivering, or managing.

Examples:

- *Annual Planning Retreat*
- *Client: Johnson Account*
- *Website Redesign*
- *Mom's Medical Care*

Each project deserves its own space in your Action system. Inside your SOAR Board™, you'll create two distinct sections under **Actions by Project**:

- **Actions by Project (Physical):**
  For projects that include paper or tangible materials, use our proprietary *Productive Environment Finding System™*. This electronic file index makes it fast to file and easy to find, even if you have multiple drawers of paper.

- **Actions by Project (Digital):**
  For projects that exist entirely in digital form, create a bullet under **Actions by Project (Digital)** in your SOAR Board™. Organize these bullets alphabetically to make filing intuitive. And when it's time to retrieve something, just use Workflowy's search bar, no numbering required.

- **Systems, Habits & Routines:** Use this section for recurring tasks and templates. It's flexible, so as your system comes to life, you may think of other items that can go here, otherwise, you can just leave it empty for now.

⬤ Action

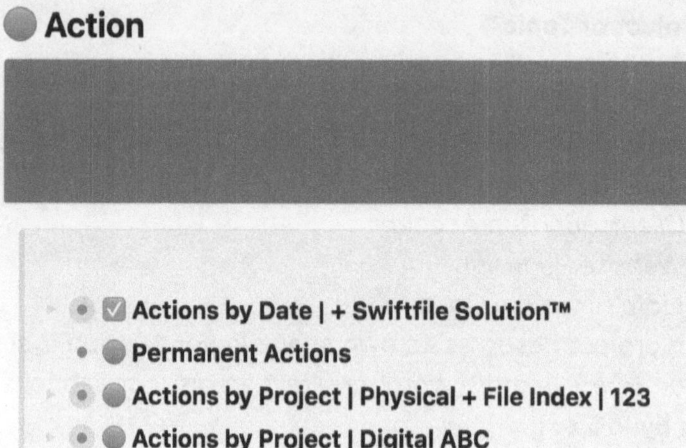

As projects are completed, archive them or move them to Reference, physically, digitally, or both.

📌 Client Snapshot: Tanya's Peace of Mind

Tanya, a graphic designer and mom of three, had Action items scattered across sticky notes, notebooks, and Trello boards.

Once she implemented her SOAR Board™, she created:

- "By Date" bullets for tasks due each week
- "Permanent Actions" for weekly work like invoicing and team discussions
- "Actions by Project" for each client she was actively working with

"I finally stopped using my brain to remember everything. Now I open my SOAR Board™, and it tells me exactly where to focus."

The Power of Placement

One of the Magic 7™ tools is your **Action System**, and it needs to be within reach.

That might mean folders in your closest desk drawer, *and* it means keeping your SOAR Board™ open as a pinned browser tab *and* mobile app. The goal is simple:

One place. One glance. One system you can trust.

If your system is out of sight or too complex, it won't support your daily work. Keep it visible, and make it easy to update.

The Swiftfile Solution™ (Date File System)

One of our most popular physical tools is the **Swiftfile Solution™**, a fast, paper-based system for keeping time-sensitive tasks and reminders organized.

It includes **43 folders**:

- 31 folders labeled **1–31** (for each day of the month)
- 12 folders labeled **January–December**

Use it to:

- File birthday cards by send date
- Drop in conference reminders or paperwork
- Create habits (like "send invoice every Friday")

This is the modern version of the classic "tickler file," and it's still one of the most effective ways to stay on track with paper-based Action items.

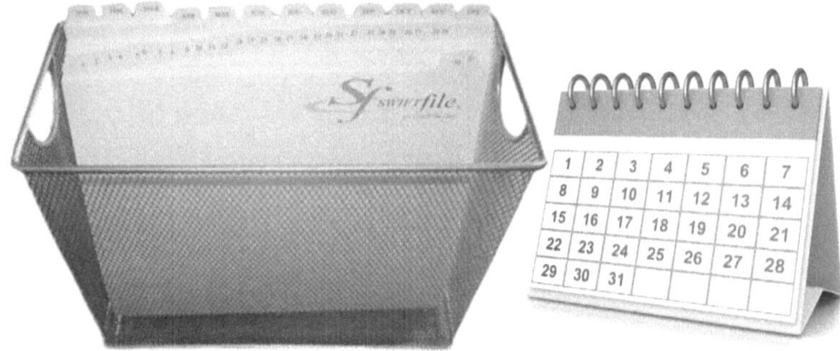

You can purchase the Swiftfile Solution™ individually at productiveenvironment.com/swiftfile.

Action Starts with Clarity

You don't need 17 productivity apps.

You need one place to track the decisions you've already made, and a reliable way to take the next step.

By organizing your Action items **by Date, by Type, and by Project**, you'll know exactly where everything lives. The clutter will start to disappear because you've finally given everything a place.

Your **SOAR Board™** becomes the bridge between information and execution.

And the result is a life where fewer things fall through the cracks... and more things get done.

Coming Up in Chapter 5

Now that your Action system is in place, it's time to tackle the information you're keeping "just in case." In the next chapter, you'll learn our signature method for filing, using the Productive Environment Finding SYSTEM™ and a digital File Index that makes lost documents a thing of the past.

Chapter 5

File

From Piled to Filed

"I can't let go of this paper... what if I need it later?"

This is the fear that fuels every overflowing inbox, teetering pile, and forgotten filing cabinet. But here's the truth: filing doesn't have to be hard, and you don't have to remember everything.

You just need a system that makes it easy to *find* what you've already decided to keep.

This chapter introduces the method we've used with thousands of clients to eliminate paper stress, reduce decision fatigue, and create filing systems they actually use **with confidence**.

From Action to Reference

By now, you've learned how to use the **ART of Organizing Information™**, and how to track your Action items using the SOAR Board™.

Now we're turning our attention to the "R" in the ART framework: **Reference**.

Reference includes anything you want to keep for future use, but don't need to act on right now.

Examples:
- Tax records
- Receipts
- Completed client projects
- Legal documents
- Insurance policies
- Workshop materials
- Product manuals
- Business licenses or certifications

If you might need to access it again, it belongs here, in your Reference system.

The Productive Environment Finding SYSTEM™

At the heart of our approach to organizing Reference information is this principle:

> **Clutter is Postponed Decisions®, and filing is the act of deciding what's worth keeping, and giving it a place to live in a way that allows you to FIND it again when you need it.**

Most filing systems fail because they rely on memory. You have to remember where you filed it, and what you called it.

But what if you didn't need to remember?

What if you could just **search**, and find exactly what you need when you need it?

That's what the **Productive Environment Finding SYSTEM™** is designed to do.

Why Traditional Filing Doesn't Work

Let's say you're looking for a receipt from your car repair.

Where would you have filed it?

Under:
- "Car"?
- "Honda"?

- "Mechanic"?
- "Repairs"?
- "Auto"?

You might not remember, and someone else certainly wouldn't.

That's the problem with filing by name, category, or alphabetical systems: they depend on consistent naming, and most people don't file the same way every time.

A Better Way: "Google for Paper"

Instead of trying to guess where a file lives, you can search for it using **keywords.**

We call this method the **Productive Environment Finding SYSTEM™**, and here's how it works:

1. Label each Reference folder with a number (Ref 1, Ref 2, Ref 3...)
2. Create a **File Index** in your SOAR Board™
3. For each numbered file, type in keywords related to the contents

That way, when you search your File Index using the keyword "Honda" or "mechanic," it shows you that it's in Ref 1, even if you forgot how you labeled it.

It's fast. It's flexible. And it grows with you.

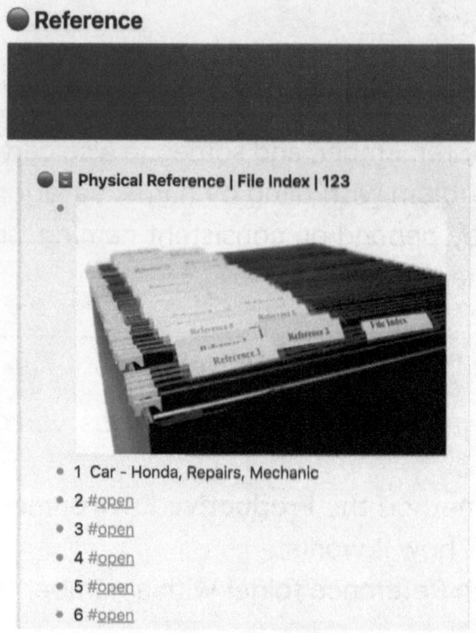

How to Set It Up (Paper + SOAR Board™)

Step 1: Gather Supplies

- 100 hanging file folders (choose one color for Reference)
- 1/5 cut plastic file tabs
- File label template

Step 2: Label the Folders

- Label folders numerically: Ref 1, Ref 2, Ref 3, and so on.

Apply the tabs using the **two-column method**:

- **Odd-numbered folders** (Ref 1, 3, 5...) get a tab on the **far left** side.
- **Even-numbered folders** (Ref 2, 4, 6...) get a tab just to the **right** of the odd row.

This creates two vertical columns that are easy to scan with your eyes and eliminate visual clutter. We do **not** recommend staggering tabs across multiple positions. This makes scanning with the eyes harder and slows down the filing process.

Step 3: Create Your File Index in the SOAR Board™

- Inside your SOAR Board™, navigate to the "Reference" section.
- Look for a bullet labeled:

  ⊜ 🔲 Physical Reference | File Index | 123

Under that bullet, list your file numbers.

Next to each one, add relevant keywords.

For example:

- Ref 1 Car - Honda, Repairs, Mechanic, receipt, Geico, oil change, warranty

These keywords are what you (or anyone you allow) can search for later to find anything related to your car.

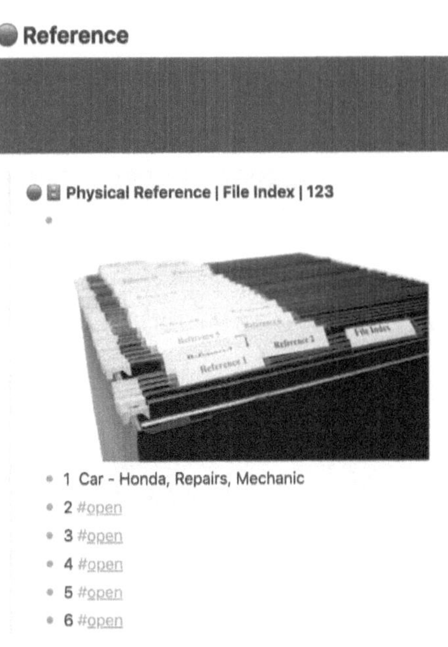

Find It Fast, File It Faster

Once your File Index is setup:
1. Pick the next open folder when you need to file something
2. Add keywords in your File Index
3. Drop the paper in the folder

Need to retrieve it? Just search your SOAR Board™.

You don't have to remember what you called it. You just type in what comes to mind, and your system will tell you where to look.

📝 Keep a printed copy of your File Index at the front of your cabinet if others will need to use it too.

Digital Reference Files? Use the Same Approach.

The ART framework applies to electronic files too.

For physical files, we use a numbered system for ease of **filing** and a File Index for ease of **finding**.

For digital files, we flip the emphasis:

- Use **alphabetical** titles for ease of filing (organizing them in the SOAR Board™)
- Use the **search bar** or view your SOAR Board™ Reference list as a master index for finding what you need

The key is to not overcomplicate your folder structure, fewer locations means faster retrieval.

And if you store digital files in multiple places (Dropbox, Google Drive, a hard drive), you can create a top-level bullet in your SOAR Board™ that links to each location and includes notes on what's stored where.

📌 Client Snapshot: Dana's Filing Confidence

Dana, a nonprofit director, had gone two years without filing anything because she "could never find what she filed."

After one week using the Productive Environment Finding SYSTEM™, she told us:

"Now I file things right away, because I trust I'll be able to find them later. That's changed everything."

Keep It Simple and Keep It Moving

You'll never get your filing system perfect. That's not the goal.

The goal is flow. The goal is to *file and find* with the least resistance.

For your physical files, keep 5–10 folders marked as "#Open" in your File Index so they're ready to assign. When something new arrives, grab the next available number, jot a few keywords, and file it. Done.

And if you empty a folder later? Mark it #Open again and reuse it.

This system isn't just more efficient. It's more human. It's unique. And it works.

For training and live setup help, be sure to join the SOAR into Action Workshop at SOARtoSuccessBook.com/Workshop.

Coming Up in Chapter 6

Now that your physical paper is under control, we're going digital. In the next chapter, you'll learn how to apply the ART framework to email, cloud storage, and other digital clutter, using The ART of Organizing Email™ and The ART of Organizing Digital Information™.

Process

From Digital Clutter to Digital Clarity

"I have thousands of unread emails, 12 folders named 'Important,' and I still can't find what I'm looking for."

If that sounds like your digital life, you are far from alone.

The volume of email, downloads, cloud documents, and shared links we manage today is overwhelming, and invisible clutter is just as exhausting as paper piles. This chapter will help you regain control and confidence, using the same tools and principles you've already started building.

We'll guide you through **The ART of Organizing Email™** and **The ART of Organizing Digital Information™**, all within the SOAR to Success System™ framework.

Clutter Is Postponed Decisions, Even Digitally

It's easy to underestimate how much our digital chaos affects our stress levels.

Unread email is postponed decisions.

Unsorted files and duplicate folders are postponed decisions.

A cluttered desktop or overloaded Google Drive... you guessed it: postponed decisions.

But order isn't about perfection, it's about trust. It's about designing a system you can trust, and using it consistently.

Let's walk through how.

The ART of Organizing Email™

Email is often the single most stressful digital tool people use.

But you don't need to obsess over "inbox zero." You just need to know what belongs where.

Every email you receive is one of three things:

- **Action** – something you need to do
- **Reference** – something to keep
- **Toss** – something you can delete or archive

This framework helps you process emails intentionally, instead of endlessly rereading the same messages.

Practical Strategies:

- **Create 2 folders or labels** in your inbox: Action and Reference. For Toss, you may simply delete, or archive the message.

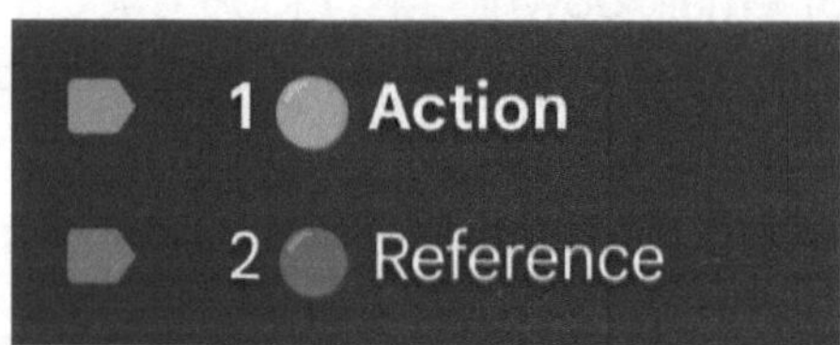

- Use your **SOAR Board™** to extract Action items and organize them by date, project, or priority
- **Batch-process email** during scheduled windows (instead of reacting throughout the day)
- **Turn off notifications** so email doesn't disrupt your flow
- **Unsubscribe** from anything that no longer adds value, newsletters, vendor promos, even that webinar you meant to attend two years ago

- We no longer recommend the popular "2-minute rule." While it can feel productive, it often leads to a full session spent on minor tasks, leaving your most important work untouched. Instead, triage email by priority. You can even add emails to your SOAR Board™ so they fit seamlessly into your Action system. Want help with decluttering thousands of emails, plus email search strategies? Our SOAR Spark program includes specific guidance for Gmail, Outlook, Apple Mail, and Office365. (https://productiveenvironment.com/soar-spark-reg).

The ART of Organizing Digital Information™

Beyond email, your digital world includes:
- Documents
- Downloads
- Spreadsheets
- Shared files
- Cloud storage
- Device folders
- Photos and multimedia

The ART framework applies here, too. The moment you encounter a file, ask:
- Is this something I need to act on?
- Is it something I want to keep for reference?
- Is it something I can delete?

Let's look at how to organize what remains.

---

1. Simplify Storage Locations

Make a list of everywhere your files currently live:
- Desktop
- Google Drive
- Dropbox
- iCloud
- "Downloads" folder
- Email attachments

Pick your preferred home base (e.g., Google Drive). Then consolidate or retire platforms you no longer use. Less is more.

---

2. Use Clear, ABC Naming Conventions

We recommend naming files using **ABC structure**, just like your digital Reference system, because your digital tools already have strong search capabilities.

Instead of starting with a date, start with a **descriptive category** that fits how your brain works.

Examples:
- Clients – Smith – Onboarding Checklist
- Finance – Receipts – 2026
- Insurance – Auto – Renewal
- Website – Blog Images – January

Your goal is easy filing and easy finding.

---

3. Leverage Search and Your SOAR Board™

Use your cloud platform's **search bar** as your first stop.

If you want to go even further, create a **Digital Reference Index** in your SOAR Board™ where you can:
- Link to important folders or documents
- Add keywords and context for shared team folders
- Jot quick notes about storage structure or login locations

Want to future-proof your storage? Include file locations, passwords (securely!), and naming conventions in your SOAR Board™.

✒ Client Snapshot: Lydia's Digital Peace

Lydia, a busy realtor with over 6,000 unread emails and dozens of scattered digital files, thought she'd "never catch up."

She created a "Reference" folder in Gmail, started capturing tasks in her SOAR Board™, and simplified her Dropbox folders using the ABC method.

"I stopped trying to fix everything at once. I just made new decisions for new emails and new files. Eventually, the clutter faded away."

Barbara's Tip: Start with What's New

"Today's Mail is tomorrow's pile™." You don't have to clean up the past. Just start organizing for your future."

Avoid getting stuck renaming or refiling thousands of old files. Instead, give yourself permission to start fresh today.

When you download something new, rename it.

When you process email, move it to Action, Reference, or Archive.

When you find something helpful, link to it in your SOAR Board™.

Progress builds quickly when your system works for *you*.

You Deserve a Digital Space That Supports You

Digital clutter creates decision fatigue, even if you don't see it.

With a few intentional habits and a SOAR Board™ that mirrors your workflow, you can stop feeling behind and start feeling supported.

Organizing your digital world isn't about being perfect. It's about being clear.

Coming Up in Chapter 7

Now that your email and digital files are flowing smoothly, it's time to protect your most valuable resource: your time. In the next chapter, we'll show you how to use the SOAR Method™ and SOAR Board™ to plan, prioritize, and protect your schedule, so you can accomplish your work and enjoy your life.

Plan

Introducing the Productive Environment Process™

Before we dive into planning your time, there's one framework you'll see throughout the rest of this book, and it's the backbone of everything we do at PEI.

It's called the Productive Environment Process™, a simple 5-step path we use to help people make progress in any area of their life or work. Whether you're organizing paper, managing digital information, starting a project, or reshaping your routines, this process gives you a dependable way forward.

The steps are:
1. State Your Vision
2. Identify Your Obstacles
3. Commit Your Resources
4. Create & Execute Your Plan
5. Sustain Your Success

You'll see this process in action in this chapter as we apply it to planning your time.

And you'll see it again in the chapters ahead, because once you learn this pattern, you can use it anywhere you feel overwhelmed or unsure where to begin.

From Scattered to Scheduled

"If I just had more time, I could finally get caught up."

It's something we hear from clients all the time, and on the surface, it makes sense. But what we've discovered after helping thousands of people is that the real breakthrough doesn't come from *getting more time*. It comes from learning how to spend the time you already have, with more clarity, intention, and structure.

This chapter is about doing just that.

You'll learn how to plan your day, week, and month using your SOAR Board™, so your priorities aren't buried in your inbox, scattered across sticky notes, or swimming in your head.

Time Doesn't Manage Itself

Time is the one resource we all have in equal measure, and it's the one most people feel like they never have enough of.

We hear things like:

- "My list never ends."
- "Everything feels urgent."
- "I'm always behind."
- "There's no space to think."
- "I never get to the important stuff."

The problem isn't a lack of effort. It's the absence of a trusted, visual system that shows you what to focus on, *and when*.

That's exactly what the PLAN step of the SOAR to Success System™ helps you create.

What Planning Actually Means

Planning isn't just making a to-do list. It's choosing, ahead of time, what you will do, *and when*.

In the SOAR Board™, planning becomes visual and intentional. You can step back and see:

- What matters most
- What's next

- What's realistic

Instead of trying to fit everything in, you start by asking: *what belongs here?*

Using the Productive Environment Process™ for Time

1. State Your Vision

What would a peaceful, productive day feel like?

What would it look like to close your laptop knowing what's done, and what's next?

Maybe you want:

- More time for client work
- Less time spent putting out fires
- Predictable blocks for deep focus
- Fewer late nights or weekend catch-ups

Start there.

2. Identify Your Obstacles

These often include:

- Constant interruptions
- Unrealistic daily task lists
- No boundaries around your time
- Trying to track everything in your head
- A disconnect between tasks and goals

You may also be overscheduled, or under-supported. Identifying the root cause helps you solve the right problem.

3. Commit Your Resources

Ask yourself:

- Do I have a calendar I check consistently?
- Do I use the SOAR Board™ as my central planning tool?
- Do I block time for review, reflection and reset?
- Is there someone I can share goals or routines with for accountability?

We don't expect you to juggle multiple disconnected tools. Instead, we guide you in building a *centralized, consistent system,* one that reflects your real priorities and is easy to maintain. That's why we recommend using the **SOAR Board™ as your home base**, with your calendar simply supporting your plans, not driving them.

4. Create and Execute Your Plan

Start here. Then structure. That's the heart of SOAR, and it applies to your time just as much as your information.

Most people try to manage their lives with task-based productivity. They make lists. They add more lists. They group tasks by category, project, priority, or importance. But when life gets full, when you're managing work, home, and multiple projects at once, task-based systems become fragile. Tasks slip through the cracks. Important steps get buried. You spend more time reorganizing your list than advancing the work that matters.

That's why the SOAR Board is built on a different foundation: time-based productivity.

2026

- Jan
  - Thu, Jan 1, 2026
  - Fri, Jan 2, 2026
    - Clear off desk
    - 2pm Meeting with Team
    - Respond to Action emails
  - Sat, Jan 3, 2026
    - Visit Farmers Market
  - Sun, Jan 4, 2026
    - 11am Church
  - Mon, Jan 5, 2026
    - 9am Meeting with Team
    - Spend 1 hour filing Reference files
  - Tue, Jan 6, 2026
  - Wed, Jan 7, 2026
  - Thu, Jan 8, 2026
  - Fri, Jan 9, 2026

Why Time-Based Systems Work Better

A timeline reflects reality. Life unfolds by minutes, hours, days, and weeks, not by categories or ideal lists. The more closely your system aligns with the way life actually moves, the less friction you experience.

Time-based productivity gives you three major advantages:

Nothing falls through the cracks.

When everything has a place in time, you're not "managing reminders." Life itself reminds you what needs attention next.

Less upkeep. Less mental overhead.

A timeline is self-regulating. You don't have to babysit a complex structure or maintain endless checklists just to keep your system functioning.

You can integrate anything.

Whatever you already know about productivity, GTD, PARA, Kanban, Eisenhower, prioritization frameworks, all of it can be folded into a time-based structure without clutter or conflict.

This is why experienced WorkFlowy users who have tried every approach under the sun eventually simplify into a timeline. It's not flashy. It's not complicated. It just works, consistently, intuitively, and with minimal admin.

How SOAR Uses Time

The SOAR Board doesn't ask you to become a time-blocking expert or build a complicated calendar. Instead, it gives you a simple structure that mirrors life's natural rhythms.

In the Actions by Date section, you'll create a clear, reliable flow for your days:

- Daily Tasks:

A focused list for each day, only the essentials. What you intend to do, not what you "should" do. This daily rhythm becomes your anchor point: a place where projects converge, decisions get made, and next steps become actionable.

By organizing tasks when they will be done instead of where they belong, your plan becomes lighter, clearer, and more honest. You always know what to do next. You always know where to put the things you can't do now. And the timeline keeps everything moving forward without forcing you to remember every detail.

- The Bottom Line

A timeline-based system isn't new, but it's rare, because most people underestimate how powerful alignment with time really is. When you move your productivity into a timeline, complexity dissolves. Overwhelm decreases. Your system becomes intuitive and self-correcting. And the SOAR Board gives you a streamlined, minimal structure to make it all work.

This is the moment your planning stops being abstract and becomes executable, one decision, one day at a time.

5. Sustain Your Success

Ask yourself regularly:

- Does this planning rhythm still work for me?
- Do I like how I'm spending my time?
- Does it work for those around me?
- Can I recover quickly when I fall off track?

Your system should serve your goals, not the other way around.

Planning with the SOAR Board™

Your SOAR Board™ becomes the visual engine for your time and task management. You can:

- Capture tasks by date, project, or person
- See upcoming commitments
- Drag and drop tasks into tomorrow or next week
- Collapse distractions and focus only on today

The beauty of this system is that it's adaptive. You don't have to reinvent your plan every morning. You just check in, adjust, and execute.

And because your SOAR Board™ lives in the cloud, you can access it from anywhere, even your phone.

📌 Client Snapshot: Nate's Calm Routine

Nate, a consultant and dad of four, said his days used to feel like a mental game of Whac-A-Mole.

Once he setup his SOAR Board™ and started blocking his week on Fridays, things shifted:

- Client projects had dedicated time slots
- Personal commitments weren't forgotten
- He stopped rewriting tasks, and just moved them forward if needed

"It's like I gave myself permission to focus on the right thing at the right time. I've never felt so on top of my work."

You Don't Have to Do It All

Productivity isn't about cramming more into your calendar.

It's about aligning your schedule with your priorities.

We've worked with people who run their entire businesses using nothing but their SOAR Board™ and a Google Calendar.

You don't need more tools, you need more trust, in your system, in your structure, and in yourself.

You now have tools to manage your time, space, and information with purpose. But systems don't exist in isolation, they're meant to support the way you work with others. In the next chapter, we'll explore how to stay connected to the clients, partners, and relationships that matter most, and how your systems can help you show up with intention instead of overwhelm.

Connect

From Disconnected to Connected

"I'm great at taking care of my clients... but terrible at keeping in touch with my friends."

Sound familiar?

Whether it's following up with leads, checking in with past clients, or remembering birthdays and thank-you notes, staying connected in today's world takes more than good intentions. It takes a system.

That's what this chapter is all about.

You'll learn how to use your SOAR Board™ and your calendar to manage one of your most valuable assets: relationships, with prospects, clients, team members, vendors, collaborators, and the people who matter most in your personal life.

Why Connection Matters

People often come to us for help organizing paper, email, and time. But what they *really* want is peace of mind, and stronger relationships.

They want:

- Clients who feel taken care of

- Vendors who respond on time
- Team members who feel supported
- Family and friends who know they matter

But without a reliable system, these things get lost in the shuffle.

Relationship Clutter Is Real

We often talk about digital or paper clutter. But relational clutter is just as exhausting. It sounds like:

- "I meant to follow up... and forgot."
- "I have all these business cards and don't know what to do with them."
- "I want to reconnect, but it's been so long."
- "I keep everything in my head and hope I remember."

It's not about caring *more*. It's about creating a framework so you don't have to rely on memory, or guilt, to stay in touch.

Using the Productive Environment Process™ to Connect

1. State Your Vision

What kind of relationships do you want to build or maintain?

- Clients who refer you?
- Partnerships that feel collaborative?
- A network that supports you personally and professionally?

Write down what connection means to *you*.

2. Identify Your Obstacles

Common ones include:

- No central place to track people
- Inconsistent follow-up habits
- Too many platforms (email, CRM, texts, social media)
- Guilt about reconnecting after a long pause
- Feeling overwhelmed by the idea of doing it "perfectly"

Sound familiar?

3. Commit Your Resources

What do you already have?

- A CRM?
- A spreadsheet of leads?
- Business cards from a conference?
- Contact groups in your phone?

What could you add?

- A bullet in your SOAR Board™ for each relationship type
- A Relationship Tracker to note dates, details, and follow-up

4. Create and Execute Your Plan

Use your SOAR Board™ to create a CONNECT section, with bullets such as:

- Clients
- Leads
- Vendors
- Referral Partners
- Friends & Family
- Team

Under each, you can create a tracker with:

- Name
- Contact method
- Date of last connection
- Notes or reminders
- Follow-up schedule

Keep it simple. The goal is visibility and consistency, not perfection.

5. Sustain Your Success

Consistency builds connection. Revisit your tracker weekly and ask:

- Who haven't I connected with lately?
- Who needs a thank-you?
- Who might need a check-in?

Over time, you'll build a rhythm, and relationships will feel lighter, not heavier.

📌 Client Snapshot: Michelle's Referral Surge

Michelle, a leadership coach, used to keep her contact info in Gmail and her follow-ups on sticky notes.

After building a simple Relationship Tracker in her SOAR Board™, she created a system to follow up with warm leads every Friday.

"Within two weeks, I booked three new clients, and didn't feel like I was 'selling.' I was just reconnecting."

What About a CRM?

If you're already using a CRM (Contact Relationship Manager), great! Think of your SOAR Board™ as your *front-end thinking space*, the bridge between your inbox, task list, and CRM.

You can use the SOAR Board™ to:

- Capture contacts during a webinar or networking event
- Track outreach related to a launch or offer
- Link to detailed profiles stored in your CRM

If you're looking for a more robust option, we recommend **PEconnect™**, our private-labeled CRM platform. It's designed for business owners and professionals who want to automate follow-up, manage leads, track client interactions, and even deliver workshops or digital content, all in one place.

For more information, email me at andrea@productiveenvironment.com with subject: CRM.

Whether you're starting with a simple Relationship Tracker or ready to implement a complete CRM, the goal is the same: create a system that supports your connections, without letting things fall through the cracks.

Barbara's Perspective: Let Your Life Be the Message

Barbara often quotes this excerpt from a poem by Edgar Guest:

*"I'd rather see a sermon than hear one any day.
I'd rather you walk with me than merely show the way."*

We teach clients to create intentional systems, not only for the sake of productivity, but as a way of showing up consistently, with care, in all areas of life.

Your systems reflect your values.

When your relationships are supported by structure, your presence becomes the message.

Coming Up in Chapter 9

Strong relationships help you stay connected to the people who matter most. But connection alone isn't enough to keep life and work running smoothly. You also need the structure to support it. That's where systems come in. Simple, repeatable processes that make it easier to follow through, reduce decision fatigue, and keep your projects moving, even when life gets busy. In the next chapter, we'll bring everything together and show you how to build a system you can trust. One that supports your work, your relationships, and your goals... all in one place.

Chapter 9

Systemize

From Random to Routine

"We don't rise to the level of our goals; we fall to the level of our systems." – James Clear

If you've ever created a beautiful plan, only to watch it fall apart after a busy week, you're not alone.

This chapter is where we bring it all together.

You've cleared the piles, processed the backlog, and started building a system. Now it's time to lock it in, by systemizing your routines, reinforcing your habits, and sustaining your SOAR Board™ as the trusted command center for your life and business.

The Purpose of SYSTEMIZE

The final phase of the SOAR to Success System™ is what turns your progress into permanence.

You've already learned to:

- Systemize and organize your space
- Create order with Action & Reference
- Build planning habits
- Begin connecting intentionally

Now you'll learn how to:
- Automate key decisions
- Turn repeated actions into routines
- Sustain your results with minimal effort
- Use your SOAR Board™ as a tool for long-term momentum

Reorganizing Is a Permanent Condition

One of the things Barbara often says is, *"Reorganizing is the permanent condition of a healthy organization."*

There will always be changes:
- A new season in your life
- A shift in your business
- A new hire
- A health challenge
- A fresh opportunity

Your system isn't meant to be rigid. It's meant to be resilient, because life isn't static, and neither is work.

Using the Productive Environment Process™ to SOAR Long-Term

1. Revisit Your Vision
- What did you want to achieve when you started this book?
- Has your vision evolved?
- What does success look like for you now?

Systemizing is about making that vision easier to live out, day by day.

2. Acknowledge New Obstacles
What's different now?
- Are you busier?
- Did something unexpected come up?
- Are you avoiding parts of the system?

Obstacle awareness isn't failure, it's feedback.

3. Refresh Your Resources

Are you using:

- The SOAR Board™ daily?
- Your planning rhythm weekly?
- Your File Index regularly?
- A digital storage system you trust?

Would a coach, CPES (Certified Productive Environment Specialist), or accountability partner help you stay on track?

You don't have to do it alone.

4. Create and Execute a Maintenance Plan

A few simple systems can help you maintain what you've built:

Weekly Planning Review

Spend 15–30 minutes reviewing:

- What got done
- What needs to move
- What's upcoming

Monthly Reset

Check:

- Your Action bullets, what's outdated?
- Your Reference areas, anything to archive?
- Your calendar, any buffer time to block?

Quarterly Strategy Review

- Revisit your original vision.
- Reinforce what's working.
- Release what's not.
- This isn't about doing *more*. It's about maintaining the structure that makes your life and business *lighter*.

📌 Client Snapshot: The Pivot That Paid Off

After using the SOAR Board™ for 6 months, Lisa, a nonprofit founder, found herself in a season of transition. Her team was growing, and her responsibilities had shifted.

Instead of scrapping everything and starting over, she adjusted:

- Archived a few personal projects

- Added a new "Team Hub" section to her Board
- Delegated recurring tasks via PEconnect™

"It only took an hour to reorganize my board, but it gave me months of clarity."

Systems Build Confidence

When your tasks, files, and relationships are structured, you no longer wonder:

- "Where did I put that?"
- "What am I forgetting?"
- "How will I keep up with this pace?"

You have a system. And that system gives you space.

To breathe.

To lead.

To create.

To rest.

That's what it means to live in a Productive Environment, an intentional setting where you can accomplish your work and enjoy your life.

Coming Up in Chapter 10

You Made It This Far. You've learned the concepts, explored the tools, and seen how the SOAR Method works. Even if you haven't taken action yet, that's ok, many people read first, then build. In the final chapter, you'll discover additional resources to help you take your first steps, create your system, and build a rhythm that helps you keep going once you start.

Chapter 10
Sustain

From Inspiration to Implementation

You've learned a new way to think about your work, your information, and your environment.

Now it's time to put the system in place and begin using it right away.

Why Sustain Matters

Using a system isn't a one-time event.
It's something you return to, day after day, week after week.

Life changes.
Priorities shift.
New demands show up.

A sustainable system doesn't prevent that.
It supports you through it.

That's why *Sustain Your Success* is the final step of the Productive Environment Process™. It's about continuing to use what works, even as your life evolves.

What Helps It Last

Lasting progress requires:
- A system you trust
- A simple rhythm
- Support when you drift

The SOAR Board™ gives you the structure.

Support helps you focus, regroup when necessary, and keep moving forward.

Barbara's Perspective

"Organizing isn't about perfection. It's about creating an environment that allows you to do what God put you on this earth to do."

Systems create space: for focus, direction, and meaningful work.

Your Next Step

To put this system into practice, your next step is to join us in the SOAR into Action Workshop™.

SOAR into Action Workshop™

Install your SOAR Board™, organize Action vs. Reference, and begin using the system right away.

☞ **SOARtoSuccessBook.com/Workshop**

From there, you can choose the level of support that fits your season, from short-term momentum to ongoing community and coaching inside the SOAR to Success Continuum.

One Last Thought

You don't have to do this alone.

When your environment supports you, everything feels lighter.

We'll be here to help you SOAR to Success. ☺

- Andrea Anderson

You're Invited to the

SOAR INTO ACTION™ WORKSHOP

THE NEXT STEP — DESIGNED TO TAKE YOU FROM LEARNING THE SYSTEM TO *USING IT IN REAL LIFE*

In this hands-on workshop, you will:

- Set up your own SOAR Board™ — with guided, step-by-step support
- Organize your Action and Reference items using the ART framework — with real examples
- Learn how to use the system daily — not perfectly, but consistently and sustainably
- Walk away with focus, confidence, and clear next steps

Ready to move from insight to action?

SOARtoSuccessBook.com/Workshop

Join our team!

Do You Have a Passion for Productivity and Helping Others Get Organized?

Inside our Certification Program, you will:

- Master the Productive Environment Process™ and the SOAR Method™
- Learn how to organize paper, digital files, email, and photos so your clients can *find anything they file in seconds*
- Build your own specialized productivity consulting business *or strengthen the one you have*
- Receive mentorship, support, and real-world client coaching opportunities
- Receive training, tools and marketing support to grow your business – *we'll build & host your first sales funnel for you!*
- Join a community of mission-driven organizers and productivity experts

Discover How to Become a <u>Certified Productive Environment Specialist</u> in 90 Days!

www.BecomeASpecialist.com